Hawaii Travel Guide

How to Travel to Hawaii Cheap

Introduction

I want to thank you and congratulate you for downloading the book, *"Hawaii Travel Guide: How To Travel to Hawaii Cheap."*

The Hawaiian Islands is a travel destination that appears on almost every person's bucket list. Often known as a luxury destination, Hawaii can very much be enjoyed on a budget. This book is a step-by-step guide for those who want to experience the paradise of the Pacific without going to financial jeopardy. This guide will show you how to find the best deals, avoid hidden costs, plan ahead, stay local, and know your destination, so you can enjoy Hawaii's tropical wonders on a budget.

Thanks again for downloading this book, I hope you enjoy it!

Contents

About Hawaii

Hawaii is the 50th state of the United States of America. It is an archipelago of nineteen volcanic islands in the Pacific Ocean, located between mainland USA and Japan. It is ethnologically considered to be part of Polynesia. Only 6 of the 19 islands are accessible to tourists.

The islands were home to native Polynesians for hundreds of years. In 1795, the islands were brought under a single monarchy called the Kingdom of Hawaii. The monarchy was in power till 1893, when rich landowners from America and Europe overthrew the king.

Hawaii became a territory of the USA in 1898 and its 50th State on 21st August 1959. "Hawaii", which is the name of the State, is not to be confused with the largest island in the archipelago which is also known as Hawaii or the Big Island. The capital of Hawaii is Honolulu, which is situated on the island of Oahu.

Visa requirements for Hawaii are the same as those for Mainland USA. American citizens do not require visa or passport to travel to Hawaii as it is considered a domestic destination. Hawaii does not follow Daylight Saving Time.

Snapshot of the main islands of Hawaii

Hawaiian Name	Nickname	Best Known For
Oahu	The Gathering Place	The capital city of Honolulu with its international airport, Pearl Harbor Waikiki Beach, Laniakea Beach, surfers' paradise, Green sea turtles
Maui	The Valley Isle	Haleakala (largest volcanic crater on earth), Iao Valley, rolling hills, whale-watching, and stunning beaches
Hawaii	The Big Island	Largest island and first arrival place of Polynesians. It has 11 climatic zones: beaches, volcanoes, snowcapped summits (Mauna Loa and Mauna Kea) and rainforests. Hawaii Volcanoes National Park, Puukohola National Historic Site, Kalapana Lava viewing area.
Kauai	The Garden Isle	Jagged cliffs and green valleys of Na Pali, popular beaches like Poipu. Waimea Canon known as the Grand Canyon of the Pacific
Molokai	The Friendly Isle	Home to well-preserved Hawaiian culture with the majority of the population being of Polynesian descent. It has the highest sea cliffs in the world.
Lanai	The Pineapple Isle	A pineapple plantation in the past, now it is a 98% privately-owned island with expansive golf courses, a few luxury resorts and no traffic lights

Culture

One man's tourist destination is another man's home, so here are a few insights into Hawaii's culture and sensitivities for a better connect.

Aloha- is a Hawaiian greeting to say "hello" or "goodbye". The expression means peace and love. Hawaii is often nicknamed as the *Aloha State.*

Shaka (Hang loose)- is the popular Hawaiian hand gesture where the thumb and the little finger point up while the other fingers are folded to the palm, and you rotate your palm from left to right. This gesture can mean "how's it going?" or "what's up" or "all ok?" The Shaka has been adopted by surfers.

Luau- Traditional Hawaiian party complete with a feast and festivities like the Hula dance, the Lei garlands and traditional music.

Hawaiian and Local- The native Hawaiians are indigenous Polynesians. Through the ages people from different regions have settled in Hawaii including many Portuguese, Japanese, Chinese and Filipinos. A Hawaiian is a person of native Polynesian descent and a local is someone who is born in Hawaii.

Mainland- United States is referred to as *Mainland* and not as *the States* or *USA,* as Hawaii is very much a part of the United States.

Neighboring Islands- Islands neighboring Oahu are referred to as neighboring islands, since Oahu is the central hub for international flights.

Tipping- Giving a tip of 10-15% of the bill amount is the norm, much like in the Mainland.

Climate

April to October is sunny and balmy with July to September being the warmest months with temperatures ranging from 75°F–88°F. September can experience cyclonic conditions. November to March the temperatures cool down to 68°F due to the rains. Rainy season also implies rougher seas.

Each island has their own micro-climates depending on the direction of the trade winds. The eastern and northern parts (Windward coast) of the islands receive quite some rain. The western and southern parts (Leeward coast) of the islands are drier. Temperatures at some of the summits can be as low as 30°F.

Clothes and travel accessories

Pack light cotton clothes, a swimming suit, a wind breaker, sandals, a hat, hiking shoes, sun screen, insect repellent and a set of binoculars. For winter months pack an umbrella and a light sweater. If you are planning to visit Mauna Loa or Mauna Kea, then proper winter gear is advised.

Bring along your snorkeling gear, sleeping bag, a beach towel and a chain lock so you can save on rentals.

Know the Deals- Transportation, Food and Lodging

Flights from Mainland USA

The money spent on plane tickets is usually the biggest portion of your budget. A round trip (with non-stop flights) from the west coast of USA to Hawaii can set you back by $380-$550, whereas direct flights from the east coast could cost you upwards of $950.

Here are a few tried and tested methods to catch a better deal:

a) Book you ticket about 100-120 days before your departure date. Statistics show that airlines usually release discounted seats during this period.

b) Avoid peak tourist seasons. The best rates to Hawaii are during off-season months which are from mid-April to mid-June and from September to early-December.

c) Avoid weekend travel. Mondays and Tuesdays often have the lowest rates.

d) If travelling from the west coast of USA, the flights with lay overs in the east coast can be cheaper than the direct flights.

e) Use the Hopper mobile app or Cheapoair.com, Priceline.com, Skyscanner or Hotwire for deals, discounts and cost comparison between airlines. Hopper analyses prices to predict the best dates for the best rates for the given airlines.

f) Check for deals on the airline websites as well. Virgin America is currently offering some great introductory prices from Los Angeles and San Francisco.

g) Hawaiian Airlines, Alaska Airlines and United Airlines offer the best connections from the Mainland to Hawaii.

Airports and Airlines

The list of airports in Hawaii:

Oahu- Honolulu international airport, Kalaeloa commuter airport
*Maui-*Kahului airport, Kapalua airport, Hana airport
Hawaii- Kona International, Hilo International, Waimea-Kohala
Kauai- Lihue airport
Molokai- Molokai airport, Kalaupapa airport
Lanai- Lanai airport

Airline Company	Origin City	Destination in Hawaii
Hawaiian Airlines	New York, San Francisco, Portland, Seattle, Sacramento, Oakland, Las Vegas, Phoenix, San Diego	Honolulu
	San Francisco, LA	Lihue, Kahului
	Oakland, LA	Kona
Alaska Airlines	Anchorage, Portland, Seattle, Bellingham, Oakland, San Diego, San Francisco, San Jose, Sacramento (no direct flights to Kona)	Honolulu, Kahului, Kona Lihue has no direct flights from Anchorage, Bellingham, Sacramento and San Francisco but there is a flight from San Jose
United Airlines	Denver, Chicago, LA, San Francisco	Lihue, Kona and Hilo, Kahului
	Denver, Chicago, LA, San Francisco, Newark, Washington-Dulles	Honolulu
American Airlines	LA, Phoenix	Kona, Lihue
	LA, Phoenix, Dallas	Honolulu, Kahului
Virgin America	LA, San Francisco	Honolulu and Kahului (flights from LA are scheduled to begin from June 2016)
Delta Airlines	Seattle, LA, Atlanta	Honolulu
	LA, Seattle	Kona
	Los Angeles	Lihue

Inter-Island Flights

Hawaiian Airlines, Island Air and Mokulele Airlines are the three main airlines operating inter-island flights. Island Air and Mokulele often have cheaper fares than Hawaiian but their baggage allowance is very stringent. Mokulele does not have the best track record for punctuality. You can land up paying dearly for unforeseen delays. Most of the inter-island flights go via Honolulu airport.

To reduce your cost, it is best to choose an island that has direct flight to/from Honolulu. Inter-island flights range from $160 to $250 for a round trip.

Renting a Car

Very few of the islands have a good network of public transportation. For tourist attractions that do not fall on the bus route, you could rent a car, but do keep in mind a few key points to avoid nasty surprises or unnecessary expenses. It is fairly easy to rent a car in any of the islands of Hawaii.

a) The most popular and affordable rates are offered by Discount, Alamo, Dollar and Enterprise companies. The prices range from $30-$45 per day.

b) Bid for a car through websites like Priceline.com or BetterBidding.com. If you are lucky, particularly during low season, you could get a car for $10/day (exclusive of taxes).

c) Verify what the fees include because in some islands the taxes are not included in the prices they advertise. Taxes can cost you to 40% of the car rent amount.

d) An additional driver or passenger may attract an extra cost. It is best to verify before you rent.

e) A surcharge of $25/day for underage drivers (21-25 years old) applies in whole of the State.

Airport Shuttle Services

Roberts Hawaii offers Express Shuttle services from the main airports of all the major islands, to several hotels, resorts, hostels and lodgings. Their prices range from $10-$45 per person based on the distance.

Lodging

Camping is a great and affordable option in Hawaii, but requires some planning ahead. There are several National and State parks with basic to fully-equipped camping facilities. Permits need to be reserved in advance and cost about $5 per person or $20 per campsite for 5 people.

Vacation rentals is ideal for those travelling in a group and staying longer than 3 nights. Try Homeaway.com and Vrbo.com and you may just get an apartment for 4 people at $120 per night.

Airbnb often has good and affordable lodging options. Do read the house rules, cancellation rules and cleaning fee details before reserving.

For getting good deals on hotels search on GoSeek, Priceline, Hotwire and Booking.com

Food

Stocking up on groceries and cooking in the common kitchen of your hostel or lodging, is a great way to limit the variables in your budget. Hawaii has a handful of ABC stores, Seven Elevens, Foodland delis and Costco for your groceries as well as take-away sandwiches and coffee for $5. You can also try "plate lunches" served at many local restaurants for $10. They often include *Kalua* pork or *shoyu* chicken, with rice and macaroni salad.

Zooming in to the islands

Oahu

Oahu is the most popular and populous island of Hawaii and also its financial, commercial and tourist hub. More than 85% of the State's population live on this island. It is of no surprise that Oahu is amongst the most expensive islands with the most modern infra-structure. Honolulu International Airport receives flights from all over the world and it is the main flight hub of Hawaii. Both the International Airport and the Commuter Airport offer frequent inter-island flights. Inter-airport transfers can be done by using the free shuttle known as Wiki-Wiki.

Public Transport

TheBus is the public bus transportation system and it is one of the best in the USA. TheBus has a pretty extensive network and connects different towns and attractions of Oahu. Tickets are available in ABC and 7/11 stores.

Standard Fares are $2.50/ adult and $1.25/youth (5-17 years old). For Passes and discounts visit TheBus website. From the airport, use TheBus to get to your destination. Number 19 and 20 will take you to Waikiki beach.

There are *Free Shopping Shuttles* (trams) that take from near Waikiki beach to Ala Moana shopping center.

Top Attractions & Activities – Below 10$ and on TheBus route

Pearl Harbor –Visit the USS Arizona National Memorial, part of the World War II Valor in the National Pacific Monument at Pearl Harbor. There is a 75-minute solemn tour including a short video on the events related to WW II. There is a *walk-in Ticket* option or an advance online booking option. For the walk-in option, it is advised that you reach the Pearl Harbor Visitor's Center before 7.00a.m as queues can be long. There is a reservation convenience fee of $1.50/person.

Diamond Head –An hour long trek to reach the summit of a volcanic tuff cone and see a large volcanic crater. It is a favorite among tourists. Entrance fee is $1.

Whale-watching -From December to mid-April, humpback whales can be seen on the east coasts of Oahu. Carry a pair of binoculars and use the Makapuu Lighthouse Trail to catch a glimpse of the giant whales.

Turtle watching –The rare Green sea turtles can be seen swimming onto the shores at Turtle beach and Laniakea beach. Best time to see the turtles is at low tide during summer months.

Catch a spectacular sunset at the Sunset Beach.

<u>Dole Plantation</u> –It is the pineapple plantation that was once synonymous to the island. For $6/adult and $4/child you can partake in the world's largest maze (Pineapple Garden Maze).

Banzai Pipeline Beach and Waimea Beach –Famous for its giant waves (sometimes soaring 30ft high) and the professional surfers that artfully ride them.

Experience Hawaiian culture at Waikiki (Kuhio Beach Park) -On Tuesday, Thursday and Saturday evenings (6.00 or 6.30p.m), you can watch Hula dancers swaying to local music along with a torch lighting ceremony. Tickets are not required.

<u>Byodo-In Temple</u>, *Kaneohe*–It is a brick red Japanese style temple dedicated to Lord Buddha and a true spot for solace. Entrance- $3/adult.

Waimanalo Bay Beach Park has 5 miles of white sandy beach, bordered with ironwood pine trees, making it a scenic spot for a picnic and lazing around.

Tour the island -Take bus 52 (Wahiawa-Circle Isle) from Ala Moana to North Shore for the Leeward views of the island. Then take the 55 (Honolulu-Ala Moana) for the windward coast view. Each ride is $2.50.

Stay & Eat

<u>The Beach Waikiki Hostel</u> offers mixed dorms from $35/person/night.

<u>Hosteling International</u> offers mixed dorms from $33/person/night

Polynesian hostel Beach club has 8 bedroom mixed dorms starting at $25/person/night. Female dorms with 2 beds are priced at $37.5/person/night.

For local eats:

<u>Haili's Hawaiian foods</u> serves authentic Hawaiian cuisine for $10.

Heeia Pier general store and deli, Kaneohe serves Guava chicken burger for $6.50

<u>Zippy's</u> at Ala Moana and other locations in the island offer superb Hawaiian fast food for $8-$10 a plate. They are usually open 24hrs.

Maui

This is the 2nd most popular island of Hawaii and its 2nd largest. Maui is part of the Maui County that consists of 5 islands: The Magic Isles (Maui, Lanai and Molokai) and two uninhabited islands of Kaholawe, Molokini. Maui is known for its beautiful beaches and coastline, whale-watching, rolling hills and deep valleys, the world's largest volcanic crater (Haleakala), golf resorts, luxury condos and shopping.

Maui has 3 airports. The main airport is Kahului on the north-east coast and the other two commuter airports are in Hana on the east coast, and in Kapalua on the west coast. There are only 2 bus routes from Kahului airport which are The Upcountry and Haiku Islander routes. Fare is $2/person.

Public Transport

The Maui Public Transit System, covers 13 routes. It is not an extensive network and therefore many tourists prefer renting cars. Tickets are $2 per ride.

Rent a Scooter

Maui Scooter Shack is the ideal place to rent scooters. The rental fee is $45 inclusive of taxes for 24 hours.

Top Attractions & Activities- $10 or less

Haleakala National Park is located in Upcountry Maui and covers an area of 33,265 acres. Entrance fee is $8 per person.

- Haleakala volcanic crater is the main attraction. Located at the summit, the crater is the largest in the world. Watching the sunset and sunrise from the summit is an unforgettable experience. Temperatures can be freezing.

- Seven Sacred Pools of Oheo-Gulch Valley- This is most popular site in East Maui. The valley is deep with streaming waterfalls, fresh-water pools, bamboo forests and ocean views.

Iao Valley State Park is part of the West Maui Forest Reserve Zone, it is lush green and has a beautiful botanical garden. The end of trail gives a great view of the Iao Needle (a ridge that rises 1200ft up from the valley floor). Parking fee is $5.

Whale-watching -Lahaina beach offers the best experience for watching the great Humpback whales at play. Boat tours charge $30 for an hour's ride into the ocean. To watch for free, bring a pair of binoculars and head to DT Fleming Beach Park, 1.6miles from Napili Kai (the last stop on the Napili Islander). Or try the popular McGregor Point Lookout & Lighthouse (Papawai Point). Best time to see the whales are from November to April.

The *81 beaches of Maui* all have free entrance. Watching the spectacular sunsets from any of the beaches on the west coast is priceless.

- The most popular beaches are Lahaina, Honolua bay (well-known for snorkeling) and Kapalua bay. Kapaula is amongst the prettiest beaches of Maui with turquoise blue water and white sand. It's on the Napili Islander bus route.

- Kaanapali is close to Whaler's village on the west coast. It has easy parking, bus access and plenty of restaurants and stores.

- Baldwin Beach Park has calm waters and sprawling sandy beaches. It has a natural reef making it easy to swim and body-surf. It's on the Haiku Islander bus route.

To rent beach supplies, visit <u>The Snorkel Store</u> in Lahaina offers snorkel gear for $10/ day, beach chair-$5/day and boogie boards for $10/day. The store offers great discounts for weekly rent.

Lahaina Banyan court –It's a 141-year old Indian Banyan tree stretching over almost an acre, offering a beautiful spot to sit and relax. The local art and crafts fair takes place every second and fourth weekend of the month. It's on Use Lahaina Village route, wharf cinema stop.

<u>Friday Town parties</u> -Maui comes alive with town parties on Friday nights. Anyone can join in.

Stay & Eat

<u>*Northshore hostel*</u> has dorms for $29 per person per night. Private rooms for two costs $79.

<u>*Banana Beach Hostel*</u> charges $41 per person per night in a dorm.

Both hostels are accessible by bus.

Lahaina Inn (by the beach) offers a double room two 2 people at $110 per night. Book via <u>Booking.com</u> for the best deals.

List of popular joints that serve affordable dishes at $10 or less for a meal.

- Cannery Mall Food Court, Lahaina

- Queen Ka'ahumanu Center's food court, Kahului

- Foodland Supermarket Deli, Lahaina and Kihei

- Jawz Fish Tacos, Kihei

Lanai

Lanai and Molokai are the smaller islands near Maui. Neither have direct flights from the Mainland but there are a few Inter-island flights from Honolulu.

You can also use the ferry services from Maui to each of these two islands:

- Daily <u>Ferry</u> from Maui to Lanai takes about 50 minutes and costs $25 per adult per way.

Lanai is small with limited public transportation. To drive around, a 4-wheel drive is advised and it could cost you $139 per day. Lanai is a difficult destination to explore on a tight budget. To read more about Lanai visit <u>GoHawaii</u> which is the State's official tourism website.

Molokai

The island is fairly untouched by tourist infrastructure. Friendly Hawaiians form the majority of the population who continue preserve their native culture and heritage. Renting a car maybe expensive (~$45 plus taxes for a four seater), and it is the prefect reason for budget travelers to sit back, enjoy the sea and the sun and get to know the Hawaiian people.

Molokai has one main airport and weekly ferry services from Maui to Molokai takes 105 minutes and costs $58 per adult per ride.

Top free things to do

Molokai cliffs - The tallest cliffs in the world reaching a height of 3200ft tall before dropping into the sea. The most affordable way to see this grand landscape is from a distance from Palaau State Park. There is no entrance fee for the park. You can camp and permits cost $12 for a camping site for 6 people.

As for beaches, you can snorkel and scuba dive at Murphy's beach which is just east of Kaunakakai. The beach has clear waters and a natural barrier reef. Or a long walk on the Papohaku beach, the longest white sand beach of Hawaii, can be great to relax and unwind.

Stay & Eat

To experience a true Hawaiian town with Hawaiian houses, stay at Kaunakakai.

Aahi Place -A fully equipped B&B that charges $75 plus 11.25% taxes per night for a room for two people, including breakfast.

Hotel Molokai and Castle Molokai offers a double room for about $150 per night for two people. You can book via Booking.com.

Camping on the beaches is a good and cheap option if you bring your own tent. But only a couple of beaches have free showers and you may not get restrooms.

For Food you must try the Molokai bread from Kanemitsu's bakery that has tasty local bakes at affordable prices. For groceries and take-away lunches, the Neighborhood Store offers pocket-friendly meal options.

Hawaii, the Big Island

This is the largest island in the archipelago, and it has 11 of the 13 climatic zones of the world. It is also where Polynesians first set foot in Hawaii. The Big Island has some of the best preserved remnants of its native history and culture. It is known for its extremely popular annual festival, Merrie Monarch. Every year tourists come to witness the brilliant performances of Hawaiian art, dance and music. It takes place from 27th March till 2nd April and is considered a mini peak tourist season.

There are two main airports in Hawaii, Kona on the western side and Hilo on the eastern side.

Public Transportation

Hele-On bus network has routes catering mainly to residents who commute between work and home, and therefore does not always stop at tourist attractions. The ticket fare is $2 per ride.

Hele-On Shared Taxi Program provides share taxi options up to 9 miles per ride in the Hilo urbanized area. The shared taxi fare could be as less as $2 per ride. Coupons have to be purchased from the Mass Transit Agency or reserved online and mail delivered.

Hitchhiking is quite a popular with backpackers. Though crime rate is low, hitchhiking is not advised for single women travelers.

Top Attractions and Activities under $10

Akaka Waterfalls in Akaka State Park is a rainforest with lush greenery, wild orchids, tall trees and home to the magnificent 100ft waterfalls. Entrance Fee: $1 per person or $5 for a car.

Pu'uhonua o Honaunau National Historical Park Located in Honaunau Bay, this 180 acre historical park was the sacred place of ancient Hawaiian law-breakers escaping from death. The site includes an ancient Heiau (temple), a great wall, imposing Tikis and the Royal Grounds, home of the erstwhile chiefs. Entrance is $5 per car.

Kalapana Lava viewing -Nestled in the Puna region of the island. Here you witness actual lava flowing. Dress appropriately as it gets very hot and stay far from the lava. There is no entrance fee.

Hawaii Volcanoes National Park -Home to two active volcanoes, Kilauea and Mauna Loa this is a must-visit. The visitor's center at the park provides information on different trails and attractions. Entrance fee is $10 per person or $15 per vehicle.

- Mauna Loa is the largest volcano on earth. You have to drive up a 17 mile road to reach the Weather Observatory (11,141ft elevation) and then hike up to the summit.

- Puu Loa Petroglyphs are ancient rock drawings or motifs. Puu Loa has 23,000 such motifs (the largest collection in whole of Polynesia).

Mauna Kea is a dormant volcano and the only place in the world where you can drive from the sea level to a summit nearly 14,000ft above in two hours. Arriving at the summit is an unforgettable experience with spectacular sunsets. There is an observatory though not open to visitors. Telescopes are available for star-gazing. It is important to check for safety and weather updates at the Visitor's center, situated half way up the mountain. Entrance is free.

Hapuna white sand beach, west coast -This white sandy and very popular for snorkeling.

Papakolea green sand beach -There are not too many places in the world where you can find green colored sand. The color is a result of green crystals called olivine which are found in lava that accumulated over the years on the beach.

Punaluu black sand beach -The black color is due to the basalt from the lava had flowed into the sea. This is a great beach for snorkeling and spotting the endangered Hawksbill and Green turtles.

Stay & Eat

Pineapple Park Hostel–The hostel has two branches, one in Kona (west coast) and the other near the Volcanoes national park on the east. A bed in a dorm costs $30 plus taxes per person per night.

Hilo Bay hostel -It is located in the heart of downtown Hilo. Cost for a dorm per night and per person is $30 including taxes.

Kona Tiki Hotel situated on the Kailua- Kona beach front charges $108 plus taxes for a deluxe double room for two people.

Try local delicacies at Farmer's market in Hilo (Mamo Street and Kamehameha Avenue) on Wednesdays and Saturdays. Don't miss drinking and eating at the Kona Brewing pub. Beer is at $5 a pint and appetizers start from $7.

Kauai

The oldest island in state of Hawaii, Kauai offers lush greenery, cascading waterfalls, an awe-inspiring Canyon, some pristine beaches, Hawaiian village life and a travel back in time. The island is small and it takes about 2.5 hours to drive around most of the island. For several decades this island was untouched by tourism and the lack of sky-high hotels and crowded infrastructure is what makes it such a desirable destination.

Luhei is the capital city and has an airport that receives direct flights from Vancouver and major west coast cities of Mainland. From the airport, there is a public bus that stops at Lihue courthouse in downtown. Fare is $0.5 per person, but large baggage is not allowed.

Rent a car or scooter from Kauai Car and Scooter Rental. Their prices are very attractive at $25 including taxes (excluding underage surcharge) for a basic 4 seater car. Scooter rental charge is $49 per day.

Public transport

The Kauai Bus network connects the towns of Kekaha, Koloa, Hanalei, Kapaa/Kapahi, Lihue and Wailua. The bus has a Fixed Route and a Paratransit (Door-to-Door) service for people with special needs. The service is from Monday through Saturday. Fares are $2 per trip for adults and $1 for youths and special discounts apply for senior citizens and special need passengers.

Top Attractions for $10 or less

Na pali Coast -Known as the jewel of Kauai, the coast is lined with a range of tall cliffs and deep valleys colored in red and green hues. This is a must-see destination and must be attempted when even on a budget. The coastal waters is home to sea turtles, Humpback whales (during season) and dolphins.

The free but tough option is to hike for 11 miles on the rugged terrain of the Kalalua Trail (that crosses the five valleys of Na Pali) in a single day. Or you could attempt the slightly easier 8 mile loop via Hanakapi'ai Falls.

Waimea canyon -Situated at the heart of the island, this deep, colorful gorge has earned the nick-name of *Grand Canyon of the Pacific*. It is 10 miles long and 3000ft deep and part of the amazing Waimea State Park.

Kalalau Lookout and Pu'u o Kila Lookout -The drive up to the Canyon leads to the Kokee State park, which is a lush green park with a museum and two great viewing points. If weather permits, you can see the magnificent vistas of Kalalau Valley from these lookouts.

Neither State Parks have entrance fees.

Poipu Beach - Often topped the world's best list. It is a white sandy beach that form three crescent-like mini beaches against the turquoise waters of the west coast. This beach has

Wailua River State park - Home to the Wailua river (Hawaii's only navigable river) this park boasts of gorgeous greenery, the Wailua complex of Heiaus and the cascading Opaekka waterfalls, which you can see from the access road. There is no entry fee to the State Park but if you want a boat tour of the river, there is a charge of $16 per person

Kilauea Lighthouse and Wildlife Refuge stands at Kilauea point at the very edge of the island offering great views of the ocean and the island's nautical birds. The entrance fee is $5.

Stay & Eat

Kauai Beach house hostel, Kapaa has dorms for $34 per person per night. Private rooms for two people cost $75 per night.

Honuea Hostel in Kaapa charge $30 per person per night for mixed dorms and female dorms. Private rooms cost $75 per night.

Rosewood Kauai, Kaapa offer twin room accommodation including a kitchenette for $85 plus taxes per night for two people.

The island's favorite food joints include:

Bubba Burgers at Hanalei, Poipu and Kaapa has great beef burger for $6.

Island Taco on Kaumualii Highway serves good and affordable Mexican food for $8.25 to $12.50 a dish.

Ono Ono Shave Ice on Kuhio Highway serves delicious shaved ice treats for $3.50.

Conclusion

Thank you again for downloading this book!

I hope this book was able to help you plan your trip to Hawaii in 2016 while saving a ton of money. You will begin to realize that Hawaiian vacations are within reach.

The next step is to pack your bags, board a flight and say *Aloha* to Hawaii.

Finally, if you enjoyed this book, then I'd like to ask you for a favor, would you be kind enough to leave a review for this book on Amazon? It'd be greatly appreciated!

Thank you and good luck!

Made in the USA
Middletown, DE
26 November 2022

16076827R00015